The Quiz Book

family

By Laurie Calkhoven
Illustrated by Amanda Haley

★ American Girl™

D0521757

Dear Reader,

Which **road trip** will lead your family to its ultimate **dream vacation?** Do your parents have any funny **family secrets?** How much do you have in common with your parents' parents? Your answers to the questions in this book will **reveal all kinds of fun and interesting facts** about your family.

You'll also find **quizzes** that will clue you in to whether or not you're a **good listener,** reveal how well you know your **siblings,** and help you think about your **family members** in totally new ways!

Are you ready to discover all kinds of **family secrets?** Grab a few pencils, gather your family around, and **try not to laugh too hard!**

Your friends at American Girl

Contents

Funny Family Secrets

What were your parents like when they were your age?
Interview a relative or family friend to find out. Then quiz your
parents to see how much they remember—or are willing to admit!

1. Nickname?   _Squish_
    Mom   Dad

2. Stuffed animal they wouldn't
    sleep without?
                            Mom   Dad

3. Best friend's name?   _Peggy_
                            Mom   Dad

4. Craziest stunt they pulled with their friends?

Snuck cookies
from kitchen
late at night

       Mom   Dad

5. TV show they stayed
up late to watch? ....
                                    Mom   Dad

6. Favorite restaurant? ....
                              Mom   Dad

7. Favorite dessert? ....
                            Mom   Dad

8. Food they had to sit at
the table for hours to finish? ....
                                        Mom   Dad

9. Song they played over and over? ....
                                              Mom

....
        Dad

10. Names of pets? ....

....
          Mom   Dad

11. Collections they had? ....
                                    Mom   Dad

12. Household chore they avoided? ....
                                            Mom   Dad

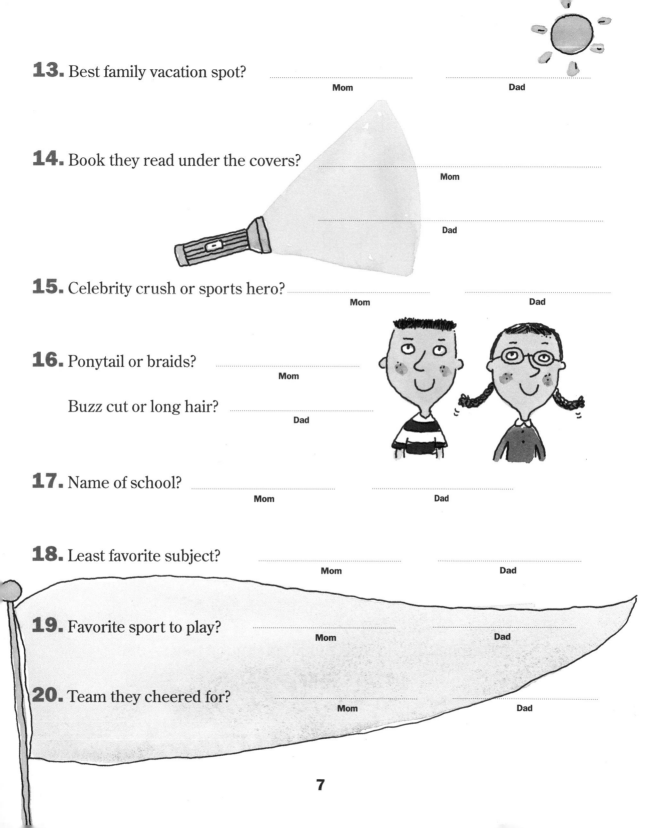

13. Best family vacation spot?

Mom   Dad

14. Book they read under the covers?

Mom

Dad

15. Celebrity crush or sports hero?

Mom   Dad

16. Ponytail or braids?

Mom

Buzz cut or long hair?

Dad

17. Name of school?

Mom   Dad

18. Least favorite subject?

Mom   Dad

19. Favorite sport to play?

Mom   Dad

20. Team they cheered for?

Mom   Dad

Family Tree

How many branches hang on your family tree?
Fill in the names of your brothers and sisters, cousins,
uncles and aunts, mom and dad, and grandparents.

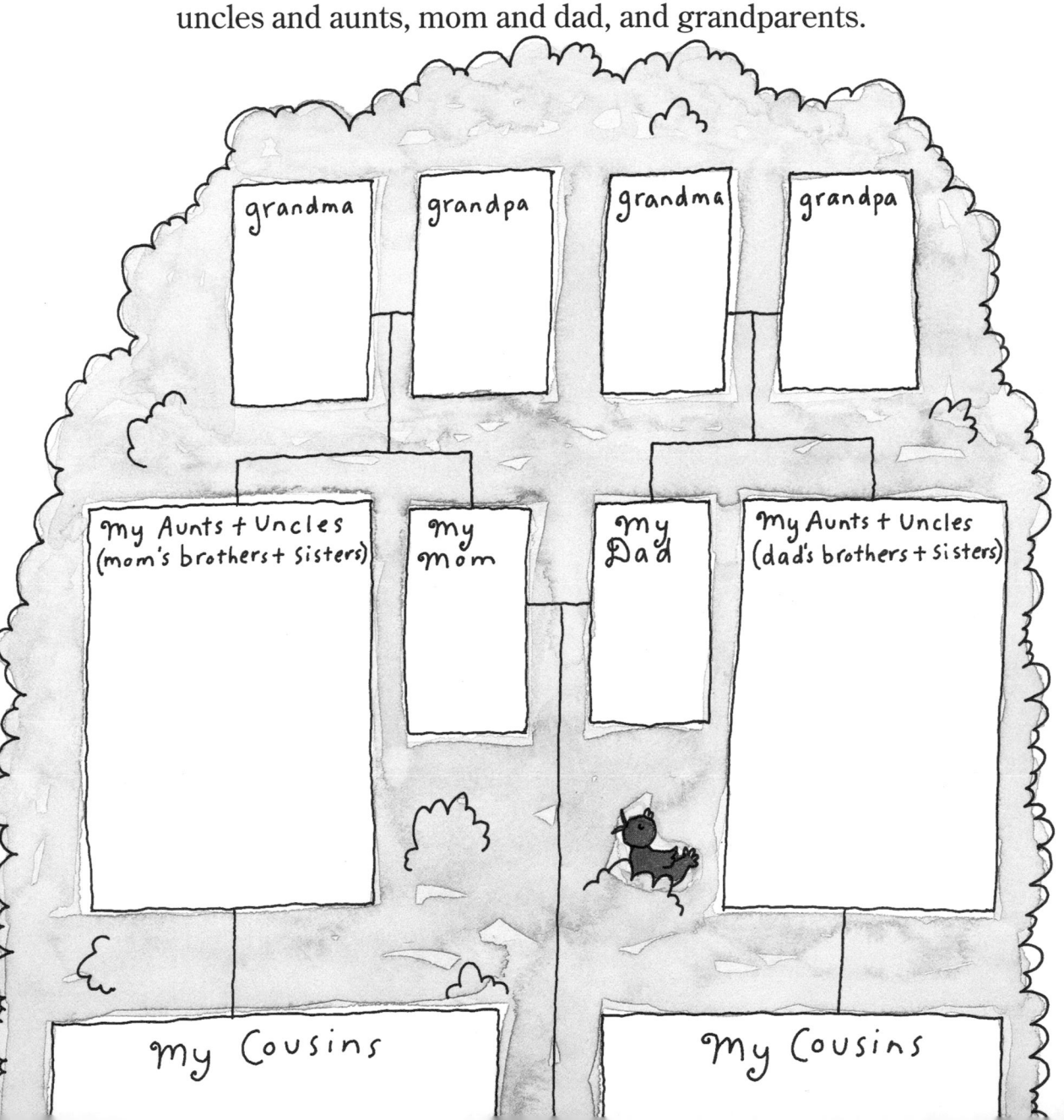

Twenty Questions

Quiz your mom, dad, older siblings, and other
family members to **find out all about baby you!**

1. Who drove your mom to the hospital? ....

2. What time of day were you born? ....

3. Were you born on your due date, or
were you an early (or late) arrival? ....

4. What was your doctor's name and
the name of the hospital? ....

5. Who visited you in the hospital? ....

6. Who picked your name and
what was it—almost? ....

7. How much hair did you have and
what color was it? ....

8. Who was your first visitor at home? ....

9. What was your first word? ....

10. Song you loved to have sung at bedtime?

11. Your favorite stuffed animal?

12. Biggest mess you made?

13. Yuck! Food you spit out?

14. How old were you for your first smile?

15. How old were you when you took
your first steps?

16. Did baths make you laugh or cry?

17. Favorite baby game?

18. Age when you slept through the night?

19. What kind of cake did you eat at
your first-birthday party?

20. First book you asked for, over and over?

Have the family members you interviewed sign their names here:

Personality Predictor

Circle the answer that best fits each person in your family.
Use a different color pen or pencil for each family member.

1. Your family invited the neighbors to a backyard pool party! What's your job?

    a. star barbecue chef ("Hamburger or hot dog?")

    b. games director ("Badminton, anyone?")

    c. greeting guests and making everyone feel at home

    d. creating one-of-a-kind invitations and decorating the yard

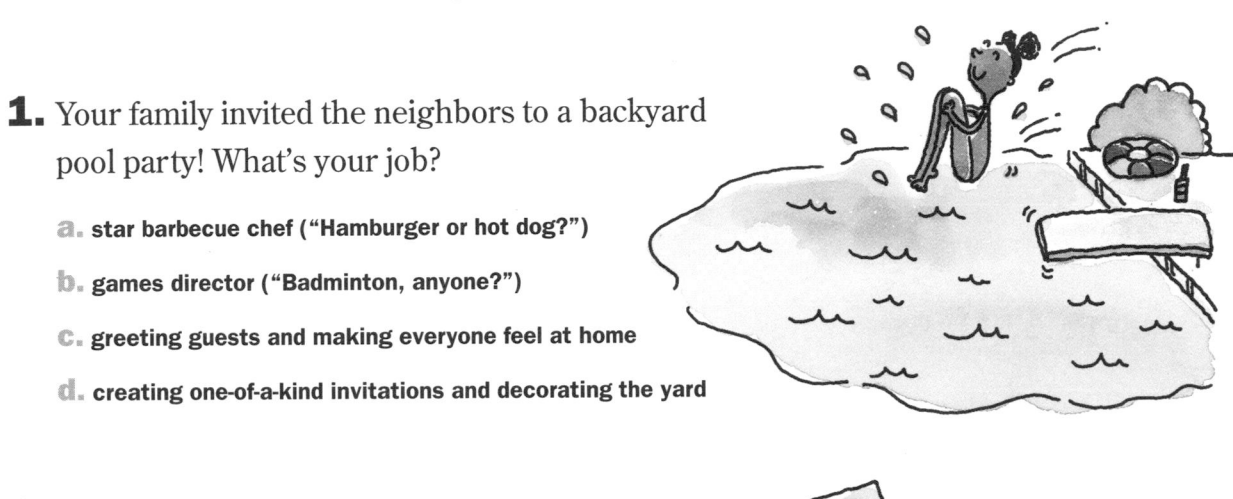

2. If your family was going on a cross-country trip, which would be your favorite mode of transportation?

    a. a minivan big enough for the whole family

    b. motor scooters (one for each family member!)

    c. a train, so no one fights over the window seat

    d. a hot-air balloon that soars above the clouds

3. Which of these is your favorite exhibit at the zoo?

    a. the lions

    b. the monkeys

    c. the seals

    d. the butterflies

4. Which of these children's books do you like best?

    a. *Oh, the Places You'll Go,* by Dr. Seuss

    b. *Where the Wild Things Are,* by Maurice Sendak

    c. *Goodnight Moon,* by Margaret Wise Brown

    d. *Harold and the Purple Crayon,* by Crockett Johnson

5. Which is your favorite beach towel?

    a. team logos

    b. bright balloons

    c. colorful flowers

    d. moons and stars

6. If you had a huge history test on Friday, you would . . .

    a. distribute study sheets to your classmates so that you'd all know what to focus on.

    b. make up songs and stories to help yourself remember all those dates and names.

    c. share your notes with your friend Nicole, who missed a week of school.

    d. eat healthy snacks and stretch between study sessions to stay alert.

7. Which of these colored tees do you like best?

    a. blue

    b. red

    c. green

    d. purple

8. On long family car trips, you . . .

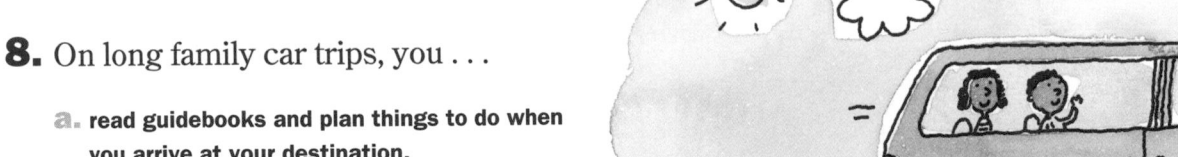

  a. read guidebooks and plan things to do when you arrive at your destination.

  b. play games and sing songs to make the ride go faster.

  c. make sure there's a cooler filled with cold drinks and car snacks.

  d. lean back and find fun shapes in the clouds.

9. It's Halloween! Which of these costumes would you choose?

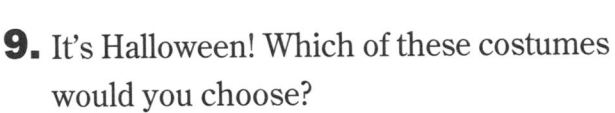

  a. a baseball player

  b. a rodeo clown

  c. a 1960s hippie

  d. a magical genie

10. Which one of these summer projects would suit you best?

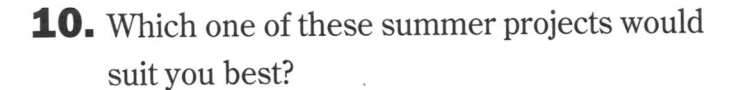

  a. starting a lawn-mowing business

  b. taking acting lessons and performing onstage

  c. going through vacation photos and creating a family scrapbook

  d. lounging in a hammock, reading all of your favorite author's books

11. Which one of these game pieces would you choose to race around a board game?

  a. a whistle

  b. a megaphone

  c. a feather

  d. a wizard hat

Answers

Mostly a's
Team Leader
You're the family member who likes to take charge. You set big goals for everyone in your family and you're not afraid to push for them. All that action means you have to be practical and organized. Your family comes first, no matter what.

Mostly b's
Family Clown
You're colorful, comical, and dramatic. When people in your family need cheering up—and even when they don't—you're the one most likely to make everybody crack up! You have a serious side, too, but if there's a chance for fun and excitement, you're at the center of the action.

Mostly c's
Family Peacemaker
You're the one who is always making sure your family is comfortable and happy. You like to look on the bright side of things and make the best of every situation, and your family recognizes all the special things you do for them.

Mostly d's
Creative Dreamer
You love to fantasize about the great things in store for your family. You're original and artistic. You probably like to spend time alone, but when it comes to your family, you're really loyal.

List your family members and their personality types here:

15

Funny Family Scale

How big is your funny bone? Take this quiz and find out if your family is **simply silly** or **seriously hilarious.**

1. You're stuck in traffic. To pass the time, your family . . .

   a. tells stories or listens to books on tape.

   b. makes up crazy song lyrics and sings them really loudly.

2. Your brother is playing in the big football game. Your family . . .

   a. shows up early for the best seats, ready to cheer on the team.

   b. paints your faces in school colors and jumps up and down whenever he makes a play.

3. One of your parents just got back from a business trip. Mom or Dad . . .

   a. shares stories about the interesting people she met and the cool things she learned on the trip.

   b. cracks everyone up with his impersonations of the funny passengers on the airplane.

4. At the dinner table, your brother tells a wild story about an imaginary friend in the cafeteria. The rest of the family . . .

 a. laughs, then goes back to a discussion about the day.

 b. adds to the story with crazier and crazier episodes.

5. You're on a family camping trip and someone just told a super-scary ghost story. At lights-out, your family . . .

 a. slips into sleeping bags and tries to ignore the weird noises.

 b. scares each other silly with ghostly moans and groans.

6. It's time for the annual Family Talent Show at your community playhouse. Your family . . .

 a. sells tickets and hands out programs.

 b. performs a musical number from a Broadway show.

7. You and your siblings are studying like crazy for end-of-year tests. Your parents . . .

a. keep healthy study snacks on hand and play "You Can Do It" music in the background.

b. quiz you on important facts and help you come up with songs and poems to memorize important details.

8. Your family is having a huge crowd over for a holiday dinner. Everyone has a long list of cooking, cleaning, and holiday chores. You . . .

a. roll up your sleeves and get to it. The reward for finishing early is a trip to the ice cream parlor for banana splits!

b. get sidetracked by Saturday morning cartoons. And did someone mention banana splits?

9. When you watch videos of your most recent family reunion, you find yourselves . . .

a. remembering to send an e-mail to Uncle John.

b. laughing your heads off over Aunt Ethel's kooky dance and Grandpa's off-key singing.

Answers

Count your funny bones!

Give yourself one funny bone for every **a** and two funny bones for every **b.**

9–11 bones

Funny

Make no bones about it! Your family likes to have fun and make each other laugh, but you have a serious side, too. When there's work to be done—like homework or household chores—you finish it first and dive into fun second. But when you do dive in, you make a big splash!

12–15 bones

Funnier

If someone in your family starts joking around, the others are sure to follow. You usually know when to be serious, but when there's fun to be had, count your family in! Whether it's cheering each other on or making each other giggle, yours is a family that knows how to laugh.

16–18 bones

Funniest

Your family chooses fun over work any day. So what if your chores don't always get done exactly on time? Your family loves to laugh and is always ready to create some fun. You crack each other up—and every-one else around you, too!

Mom & Me

How well do you know each other? In one column, answer
for yourself, and in the next column take your best guess at
what your mom's answer would be. Have her do the same on
a separate piece of paper. Then see how you both did.

	Me	Mom
1. Favorite season		
2. Favorite cookie		
3. Book you'd stay up late to read		
4. Extreme sport you'd try if you dared		
5. Favorite clothing store		
6. Song you'd sing in a music competition		
7. Favorite place to swim		
8. Sundae topping that makes you drool		
9. Favorite movie star		

10. Movie you'd watch over and over

11. Animal that gives you the creeps

12. One thing you like most about yourself

13. Present you've been wishing for

14. Favorite shoes (past or present)

Answers

Score 1 point for each correct answer.

10 to 14 points

Great going! It's hard to keep up-to-date when you're running in different directions and school and work responsibilities get in the way, but you and your mom have done it. Remember to keep talking to stay in touch with each other's lives.

5 to 9 points

You and your mom know what's going on in each other's lives, but you're still discovering new things. That's part of the fun of staying connected. Plan some special mother-daughter events, like a cookie baking session or a long bike ride.

0 to 4 points

Maybe it's time to let your mom in on your life, or pay more attention to what's going on in hers. Share your news at the dinner table, talk in the car instead of listening to the radio, or plan a girls' spa night. Just think of the fun you'll have learning new things about each other.

Test Your Sib IQ

Take this quiz to find out your sibling "interest" quotient.
Then **test their IQ** about you.

1. You stumble downstairs late Saturday morning and find your whole family dressed in the high school's colors with pom-poms in hand. You say . . .

"Oh no! I overslept on the day of Brandon's big game!"

"Brandon's football game is today?"

"Since when does Brandon play football?"

2. Your older brother mentions that Kendra invited him to her birthday party. You say . . .

"Kendra? Didn't you like her last year?"

"Kendra? Never heard of her."

"That's so cool! I knew Kendra liked you!"

3. You're at the park with your little sister, when Dylan, the boy who's been picking on her all year, runs by. You . . .

invite that cute little boy over to play with your sister.

ask her if that nice boy Dylan is in her class this year.

offer to have a word with the little bully.

4. You walk by your brother's room on the way to bed and see him hunched over the books. You . . .

tell your Mom. He's not allowed to stay up this late.

say, "What's up? Oh, you have a test or something, right?"

wish him well on his history test and remind him to get a good night's sleep.

5. When your sister shows up for breakfast dressed in a poodle skirt, you say . . .

"You look great! Have a good time at '50s Day."

"I thought you liked beagles. Are you into poodles now?"

"What's with the costume? It's not Halloween."

6. Mom asks you to bring home your sister's favorite from the ice cream parlor. You . . .

ask for two scoops of Rocky Road in a cup. That's her absolute fave.

buy your own favorite. Who knows what hers is?

can't remember if it's chocolate or vanilla, so you buy both.

7. Dad's planning a surprise party for your little sister and asks for help with the guest list. You . . .

get her class list and invite all the girls—those are probably her best friends.

make a list of her friends from school and her neighborhood buddies.

swear her best friend to secrecy and ask for her help.

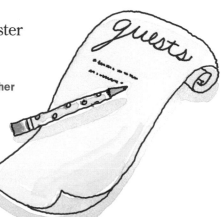

8. You run into your sister's ex-best friend, Mindy, at the mall. When Mindy asks for info about your sister, you . . .

tell her to call your sister. She's moping around at home and bringing you down.

vaguely remember something your sister said. But who cares, really?

zip your lips. No way you'll talk about your sister with Mindy.

Answers

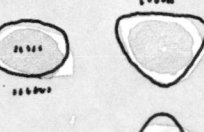

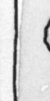
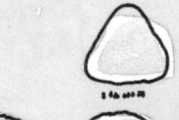

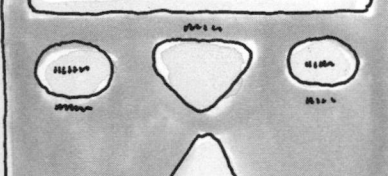
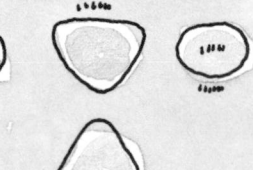

Mostly green

All Clear
Yes! You really know your sibs. Give yourself a gold star for tuning in to your brothers' and sisters' lives. You know that talking and listening are the keys to good communication, and you do both!

Mostly blue

Static on the Line
You know a little bit about what's going on with your sibs, but you could use another clue or two. Take some extra time to check in with your brothers and sisters and find out what's going on in their lives. You'll be glad you did.

Mostly pink

Tuned Out
Yikes! When it comes to your sibs, you're totally tuned out. It's time to start paying attention. Schedule some quality sibling time, and remember— it takes two to communicate.

Piggy Doodles

Draw a pig in one of the boxes below, and ask each family member to do the same. After you've "oinked" your masterpieces, turn the page to see what some people say your piggy doodle may reveal about you!

Piggy Doodle Answers

Check out the answers below to see what some people say your piggy doodles reveal about you and your family members!

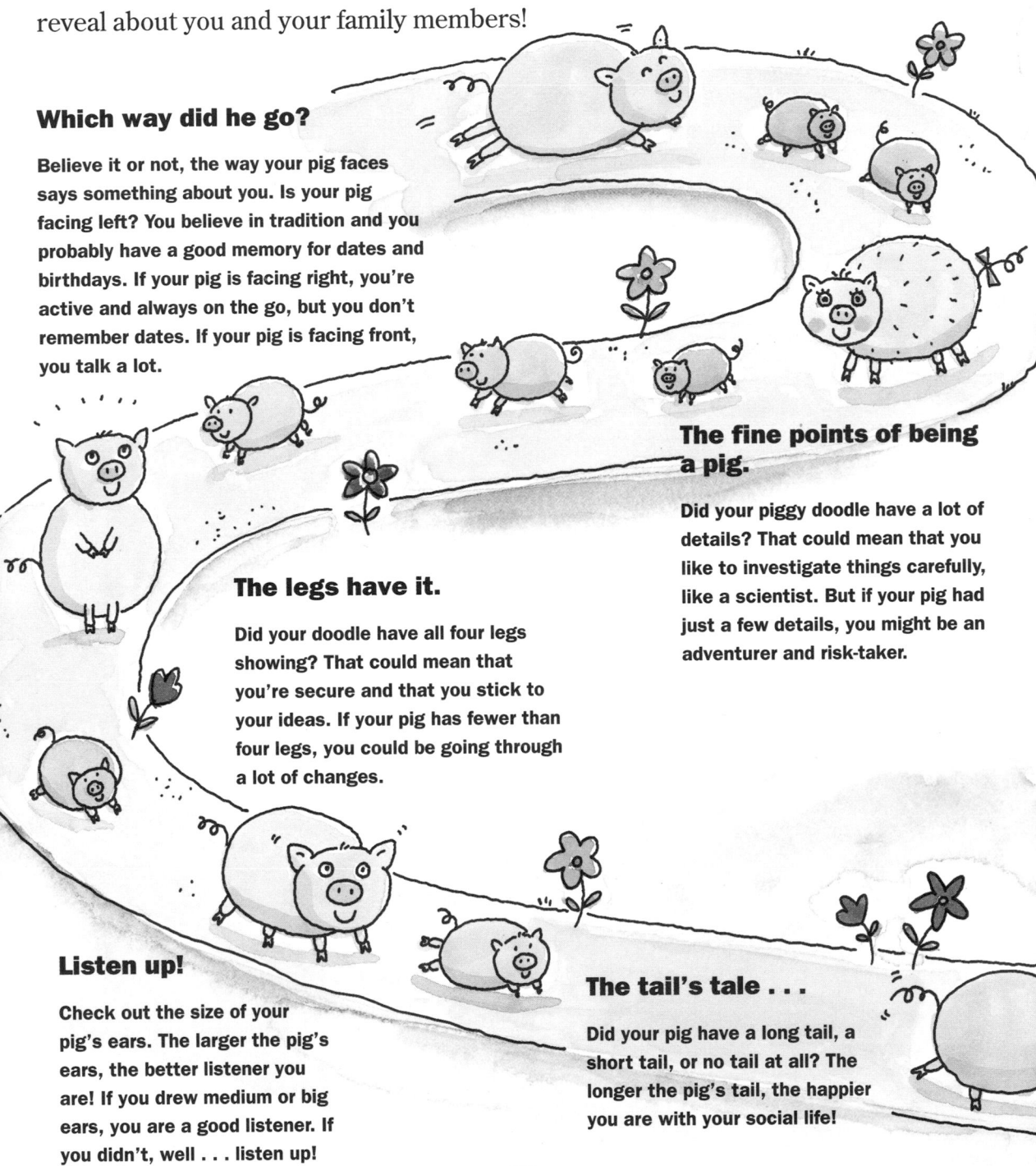

Which way did he go?

Believe it or not, the way your pig faces says something about you. Is your pig facing left? You believe in tradition and you probably have a good memory for dates and birthdays. If your pig is facing right, you're active and always on the go, but you don't remember dates. If your pig is facing front, you talk a lot.

The fine points of being a pig.

Did your piggy doodle have a lot of details? That could mean that you like to investigate things carefully, like a scientist. But if your pig had just a few details, you might be an adventurer and risk-taker.

The legs have it.

Did your doodle have all four legs showing? That could mean that you're secure and that you stick to your ideas. If your pig has fewer than four legs, you could be going through a lot of changes.

Listen up!

Check out the size of your pig's ears. The larger the pig's ears, the better listener you are! If you drew medium or big ears, you are a good listener. If you didn't, well . . . listen up!

The tail's tale . . .

Did your pig have a long tail, a short tail, or no tail at all? The longer the pig's tail, the happier you are with your social life!

A Few of
My Favorite Things

Do you have lots of sibs, a ton of cousins, or a bunch of friends? Use a separate piece of paper to list more of your favorite things!

Is it the way he **cheers you up** when you've had a bad day? Her **beautiful singing voice?** Name three of your **favorite things** about each of your siblings. Then have them do the same for you!

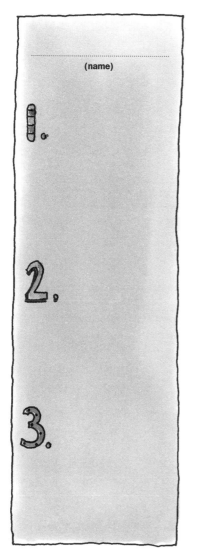

(name)

1.

2.

3.

(name)

1.

2.

3.

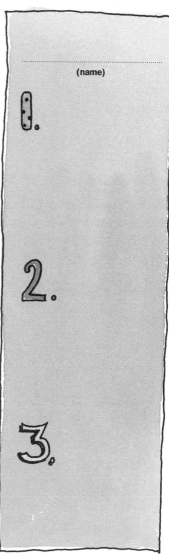

(name)

1.

2.

3.

Teammates

How well do you get along with your brothers and sisters? Do you **play fair** or **foul out?** Take this quiz and see how you do.

1. When the other one breaks a rule, who tells your parents?

a. your sib (2 points)

b. you (1 point)

2. When you and your sib both want control of the TV, who usually starts a fight?

a. you (1 point)

b. your sib (2 points)

3. You and your best bud are planning a spa sleepover, and your little sister wants in on the fun. You . . .

a. paint her face with an oatmeal mask and save your secrets for after little sis is in bed. (3 points)

b. put a "keep out" sign on your bedroom door and don't let her in. (1 point)

Keep OUT!

4. Your brother is hogging the computer again and you have to surf the Web for a homework assignment. You . . .

a. explain your problem and ask him to let you use the computer. (2 points)

b. complain to your mom and try to get him into trouble. (1 point)

E-mail

5. Your sister just made the varsity soccer team and there's cake and ice cream to celebrate. You . . .

a. make an ice cream toast, wishing her many, many goals. (3 points)

b. cross your arms and scrunch down in your seat. Who cares about soccer? (0 points)

6. Your grandparents are making a huge fuss about your brother's concert. You . . .

a. smile and agree that he's the best saxophone player ever. Your turn in the spotlight will come. (2 points)

b. pull out your last book report and show them your A+. (1 point)

7. You and your sister both sing in the choir. When the music director asks her to sing a solo, you . . .

a. jump up and down—you're so happy for her! (2 points)

b. congratulate her, but hope the next solo will be yours. (1 point)

8. It's report card day. You did fine, but your brother seems upset. You . . .

a. show him your grades but try not to gloat too much. (2 points)

b. wave your report card in his face and tell him you must have gotten the smart genes. (0 points)

9. Your mom was too busy to plan a big birthday party for you this year, but a few months later your sister has a big blowout birthday bash. You . . .

a. file the information away and remind your mom when it's time to plan next year's party. (2 points)

b. stomp your feet and cry until your mom agrees to let you have a sleepover with your friends on the same day. (1 point)

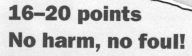

16–20 points
No harm, no foul!

You've played the sibling rivalry game and won! You're an easygoing sibling who is almost always ready to celebrate your brother's and sister's good news. Even when it doesn't exactly seem fair, you know things will even out in the end.

11–15 points
Strike one!

Everyone struggles with sibling rivalry sometimes. The next time you feel like you're Cinderella and your sibling is a wicked stepsister, take a few minutes to think about the circumstances. Try to come up with ways to make yourself feel better—without fighting—by focusing on the things you do well.

7–10 points
You're out!

Life isn't a contest between you and your sibs. Try to concentrate on you—on what you have and who you are—instead of on your siblings.

Grand Family History

How much do you know about your parents' parents? At your next family gathering, grab some **one-on-one time** with a grandparent, a great-aunt or -uncle, or an older family friend, and find out what life was like when they were your age.

1. Full name

2. Birthday (and year)

3. City or town where he/she was born

4. First language

5. Number of siblings

6. Favorite playground game

7. Best school subject

8. Favorite toy

9. Craziest hairstyle

10. Funniest clothing fad ....

11. Silliest nickname ....

12. Holiday he or she remembers best ....

13. Best childhood birthday present ....

14. Favorite kinds of books to read ....

15. President of the U.S. when
he/she was your age ....

16. Allowance he/she got ....

17. First after-school job ....

18. Favorite musical performer ....

19. Favorite radio or TV show ....

20. Clubs or teams ....

21. Year graduated from high school ....

22. Name of first sweetheart ....

23. Place where he or she met
his or her spouse ....

24. Year and place married ....

25. First thought when he/she
saw you for the very first time ....

Have the person you interviewed sign his or her name here:

....

What was the most surprising thing you learned about him or her?

....

....

....

Super Sib!?

Take this quiz with one of your siblings in mind. Take it again for each sibling, and then have them answer these questions about you.

1. You break a rule by riding your bike before doing your homework. Your sister or brother . . .

a. joins you! Homework can get done later.

b. pretends not to see you.

c. expects something in return for not telling Mom—like control of the TV.

d. calls your mom at work and tattles on you.

2. You're not exactly the most athletic kid on the block, but you decide to go out for soccer anyway. Your sibling . . .

a. calls a soccer bud and asks him to teach you some moves.

b. wishes you luck and tells you he or she will be cheering for you.

c. suggests you join the Academic Olympics Club instead.

d. tells you to get real. There's no way you'll make the team.

3. Bullies suddenly surround you on the playground. Your brother or sister . . .

a. grabs some friends and races to your side. There's no way you'll have to face those meanies alone.

b. watches from close by, ready to help if you need it.

c. looks for a playground attendant or teacher to tell.

d. heads in the other direction. Your sibling is afraid of bullies.

4. You're studying for a test in math—your hardest subject. Your sibling . . .

　a. tells you everything he or she—the famous
　　math whiz—knows.

　b. sticks around in case you need help, but waits
　　until you ask.

　c. watches TV in the same room as you—why
　　should he or she be quiet?

　d. makes fun of the trouble you're having and
　　tries to confuse you with fancy formulas.

5. You leave your diary out, opened to a page about your crush. Your sister
　or brother . . .

　a. gives you advice about how to get to know
　　your crush better.

　b. closes the book and slips it into your drawer.

　c. teases you at the dinner table that night.

　d. reads it to your crush on the school bus the
　　next day.

6. Your clarinet solo at the school concert is on the same night as your
　sibling's basketball game. Your sib . . .

　a. ditches the team to watch you play.

　b. makes you promise to play the solo again after the game.

　c. tells you how glad he or she is to not have to go to your
　　stupid concert.

　d. tries to talk your parents into skipping your concert so
　　that they can both watch him or her on the court.

7. You're in the same school as your sibling. Every time she or he sees you in the halls, your sib . . .

a. shouts "Hey!" and gives you a big hug.

b. smiles and waves.

c. waits for you to say hello first.

d. pretends you're not even there.

8. You've been super busy with your new best friend, and cancelled plans with your younger sibling—twice! Now your new friend is going to hang out at your house after school. Your little brother or sister . . .

a. plans activities for the three of you to do together, and won't take no for an answer.

b. is nice to your new friend, but gives you your space.

c. teases you and your friend until your mom makes him or her stop.

d. tries to embarrass you and drive your new friend away.

9. You borrowed your sibling's camera without asking—again. He or she . . .

a. is happy to share and hopes you got some great pictures.

b. reminds you to ask first next time.

c. asks your mom to punish you.

d. puts a lock on the closet door to make sure you can't use the camera again.

10. Your sibling got a standing ovation and a huge trophy at his or her gymnastics meet. Now you want to learn gymnastics, too. Your sib . . .

a. immediately teaches you a tumbling routine and asks your parents to sign you up for a class.

b. steers you toward a class for beginners, but offers to practice with you.

c. wonders out loud if another hobby like karate would be more fun for a clumsy kid like you.

d. threatens to quit gymnastics if you start taking lessons. Gymnastics is your sib's thing.

Check out your answers. Did you give your sib . . .

Mostly a's

Over-the-Top Sib

When you need help or support, you can always count on this sib. But sometimes he or she can be a little . . . umm . . . overbearing. It's great to have someone come to your rescue, but at times you want to ask for a helping hand first. Let your sib know that sometimes you want to stand up to that bully on your own.

Mostly b's

Super Sib

This sibling does his or her best to understand and support you, without overstepping the bounds. You can count on this sib to be there for you when you need it, and you'll do the same in return. You've both learned that siblings can be more than brothers and sisters. They can be friends, too.

Mostly c's
So-So Sib

You're not enemies, but your sibling isn't exactly your friend, either. The next time you need support or understanding, think about ways you might ask for help. If you work at improving your relationship, your sibling will, too. And the next time one of you needs a sympathetic listener, you'll know where to turn.

Mostly d's
Frightful Sib

Yikes! Your sibling is more like an enemy than a friend. It's definitely time you called a truce. Think about the things that usually make one of you mad, and talk them over when you're feeling calm instead of angry. Listen to each other's side of the story and try to come up with a peaceful solution together—no name-calling!

Circle Your Sib's Rating:

Over-the-Top Sib	**Super Sib**	**So-So Sib**	**Frightful Sib**
(My Sib's Name)			
Over-the-Top Sib	**Super Sib**	**So-So Sib**	**Frightful Sib**
(My Sib's Name)			
Over-the-Top Sib	**Super Sib**	**So-So Sib**	**Frightful Sib**
(My Name)			

Not happy with your score? Work on making your relationship better and retake the quiz in three months. How much have you improved?

Over-the-Top Sib	**Super Sib**	**So-So Sib**	**Frightful Sib**
(My Name)			

Place Your Order!

Circle the statements that make you say "That's me!"—and see where you are on the family menu. Do your answers match your real place at the family table?

You're not afraid to make decisions or to share your opinions.

You're great at seeing both sides of a problem. When friends need a referee, you help make the peace.

You're a born leader. Whether you're on the volleyball court or in the classroom, you take charge!

You like things to be organized and you're almost always on time.

You love to read and have a great mind for facts and figures.

You're determined. When it comes to meeting a goal, nothing stops you!

You love to make new friends and you're good at keeping the old ones, too.

You believe in yourself. You're super confident and you love to take on new challenges.

You love to make people laugh and be at the center of attention.

You feel like you have to work harder than other kids to get attention.

You always know where to find your books, your mom's car keys, or your brother's homework.

You sometimes feel like no one takes you seriously.

You always have plenty of hugs and kisses to give out.

You roll with the punches. If you strike out in softball, you can usually laugh it off.

Your things are yours. You're not exactly comfortable when friends ask to borrow your clothes or CDs.

You feel some pressure to be "perfect" and don't like to complain.

You're great at keeping secrets. Everyone trusts you.

You can be really critical of yourself when you miss a free throw or get a B on a test.

You're eager to please. When there's a job to be done, you're the first to volunteer.

You're good at learning from other people's mistakes.

Answers

Count up the statements you circled, and match the color you circled most to the answers below.

GUEST CHECK

Starters (reds)

You're probably the oldest child. You got to experience a lot of things first and everything you did as a baby was a huge deal. The good thing is that a lot of your parents' attention falls on you, but then so does the pressure. Even though your parents expect a lot from you, and your younger sibs count on you for advice, you're up to the challenge! Did you know? Almost all of the U.S. presidents were either first-born children or first-born sons.

Entree (purples)

You're probably the middle child. Sometimes middle children feel unnoticed. After all, they have to share their parents' attention with their older and younger sibs. But there are good things about being in the middle—you get to look up to your older sibs as role models and help out your younger brothers and sisters. That makes you super good at playing peacemaker. Middle children are usually more relaxed than their older and younger sibs. Did you know? Middle children make excellent negotiators and diplomats.

GUEST CHECK

Dessert (oranges)

You're probably the youngest child. The youngest kid naturally gets a lot of attention, but your parents can treat you like a baby for way too long. Older sibs can be great role models, but youngest children often focus on being different and trying new things. Youngest children also love to take center stage, especially if they can make people laugh. Did you know? Many actors and comedians are youngest children.

Sides (greens)

You're probably an only child. Only children spend a lot of time with grown-ups, so they tend to be just as comfortable with their teachers and their friends' parents as they are with their best buds! At the same time, only children feel a lot of pressure to be perfect and can be super critical of themselves and others. If this is you, try to ease up on yourself. Only children are used to handling responsibility. They know how to get things done! Did you know? Many only children run their own businesses.

Did we get it wrong?

Birth order is just one of the many, many things that affect who you are and how you relate to the world around you. Every family is different, and birth order gets a lot more complicated when you include stepsiblings or half siblings, or if there's a big age gap between you and your sibs. You're a unique individual, no matter when you were born.

Generation Rings

Get together with a grandparent or an older family friend and **check out** what your generations have in common!

1. On a piece of paper, write down your top ten things in one or more of the categories listed. Ask your "grand-friend" to do the same.

2. Compare your lists. Circle items you both listed, and write them in the middle of one of the sets of rings on the following pages.

3. Write the other items on your list to the side in one ring, and have your "grand-friend" list the rest of his or her items in the other ring.

Generation Ring Categories

- **Music**
- **After-school Games**
- **TV Shows**
- **Favorite Books**
- **Clubs**
- **Fashions**
- **Vacation Spots**
- **Desserts**
- **Pets**

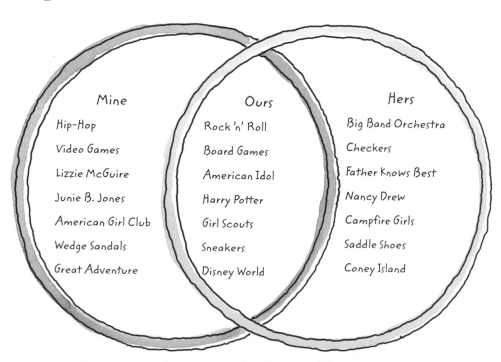

Mine	Ours	Hers
Hip-Hop	Rock 'n' Roll	Big Band Orchestra
Video Games	Board Games	Checkers
Lizzie McGuire	American Idol	Father Knows Best
Junie B. Jones	Harry Potter	Nancy Drew
American Girl Club	Girl Scouts	Campfire Girls
Wedge Sandals	Sneakers	Saddle Shoes
Great Adventure	Disney World	Coney Island

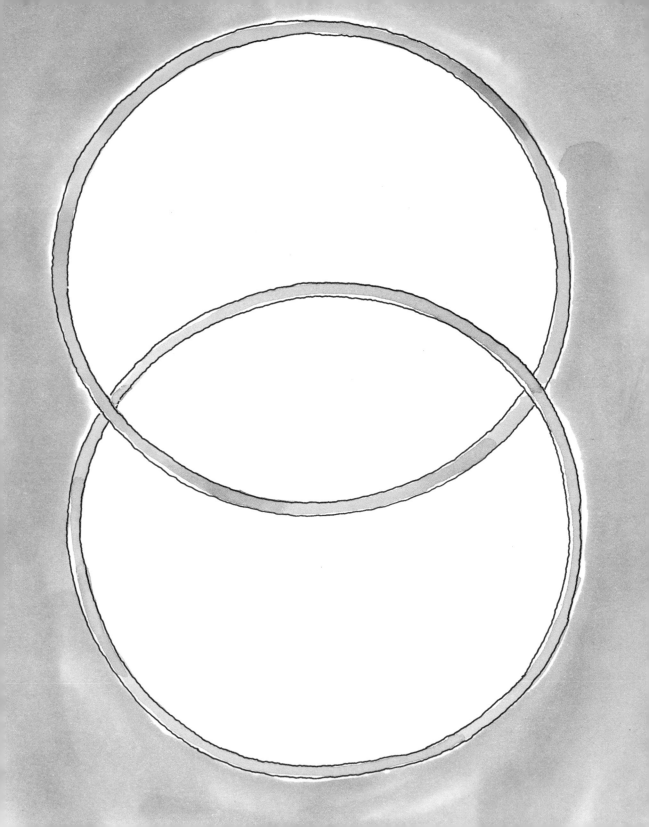

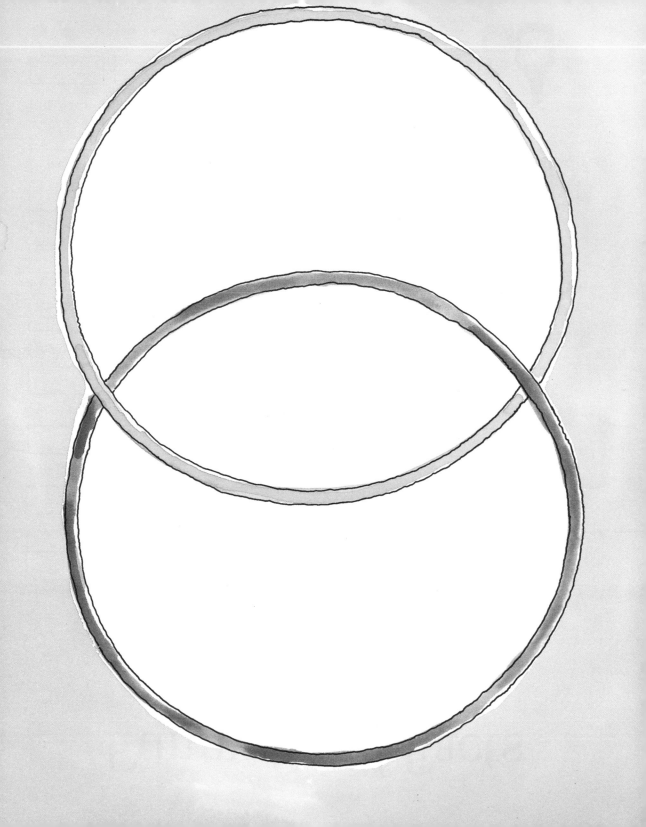

Funny Food Facts

Write your initials in a box after each statement that is **true** about you.
Make sure everyone in your family fills it out!

I've slipped food to the dog when no one was looking.

I've eaten food I dropped on the floor.

I've traded my sandwich at lunch.

I've eaten raw cookie dough right out of the bowl.

I've swallowed a bug.

I've eaten dessert before dinner.

I like cold pizza for breakfast.

I like broccoli.

I like ketchup better than mustard.

I've eaten sushi.

I like anchovies on my pizza.

I've tried vinegar on my French fries.

I've eaten an artichoke.

I've tasted sardines.

I can bake something without a recipe.

I've eaten breakfast for dinner.

I've swallowed a cherry pit.

I like cashews better than peanuts.

I like peanut butter on bananas.

I can twirl pizza dough.

I can flip an omelet without a spatula.

Dad & Daughter

Grab some quiet time to learn funny facts about each other.
In one column, answer for yourself, and in the next column
take your best guess at what your dad's answer would be.
Have him do the same on a separate piece of paper.

	Me	Dad
1. One thing you're really good at		
2. Hardest subject at school		
3. Best friend's name		
4. Favorite amusement park ride		
5. Ride you're afraid of		
6. Number of states you've visited		
7. Favorite candy bar		
8. Lucky number		
9. Cartoon character that cracks you up		

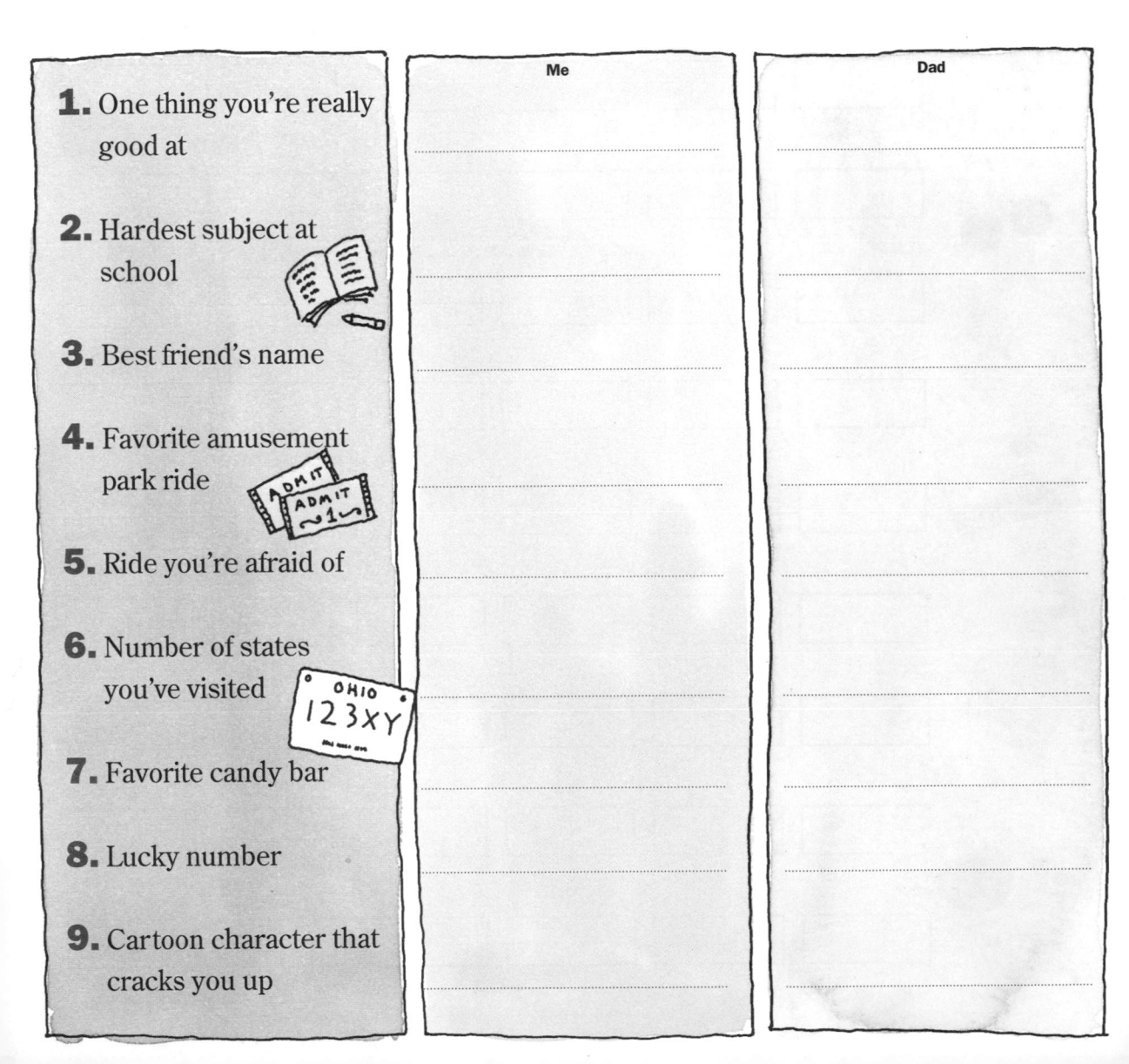

10. Birthstone

11. Favorite holiday

12. Best Halloween costume ever

13. Favorite junk food

14. Favorite TV show

Answers

Score 1 point for each correct answer.

10 to 14 points

Great going! You and your dad must be spending some quality time together. You know that when you're sharing news about your life, he's listening. Remember to keep the lines of communication open, and you'll both be happier for it.

5 to 9 points

You and your dad know what's going on in each other's lives, but you don't know everything. Cluing him in to cool new things about you can be a lot of fun. The next time you're in the car together, turn the radio off and talk instead. Or plan a special father-daughter dinner.

0 to 4 points

Maybe it's time to let your dad in on your life or learn a little about what's going on in his. Plan some fun one-on-one time, like a mini-golf challenge or a long walk in the park. Think of the fun you'll have learning new things about each other.

Family Crest

Follow these simple steps to create your family's very own coat of arms!

1. Choose an animal or bird to represent your family:

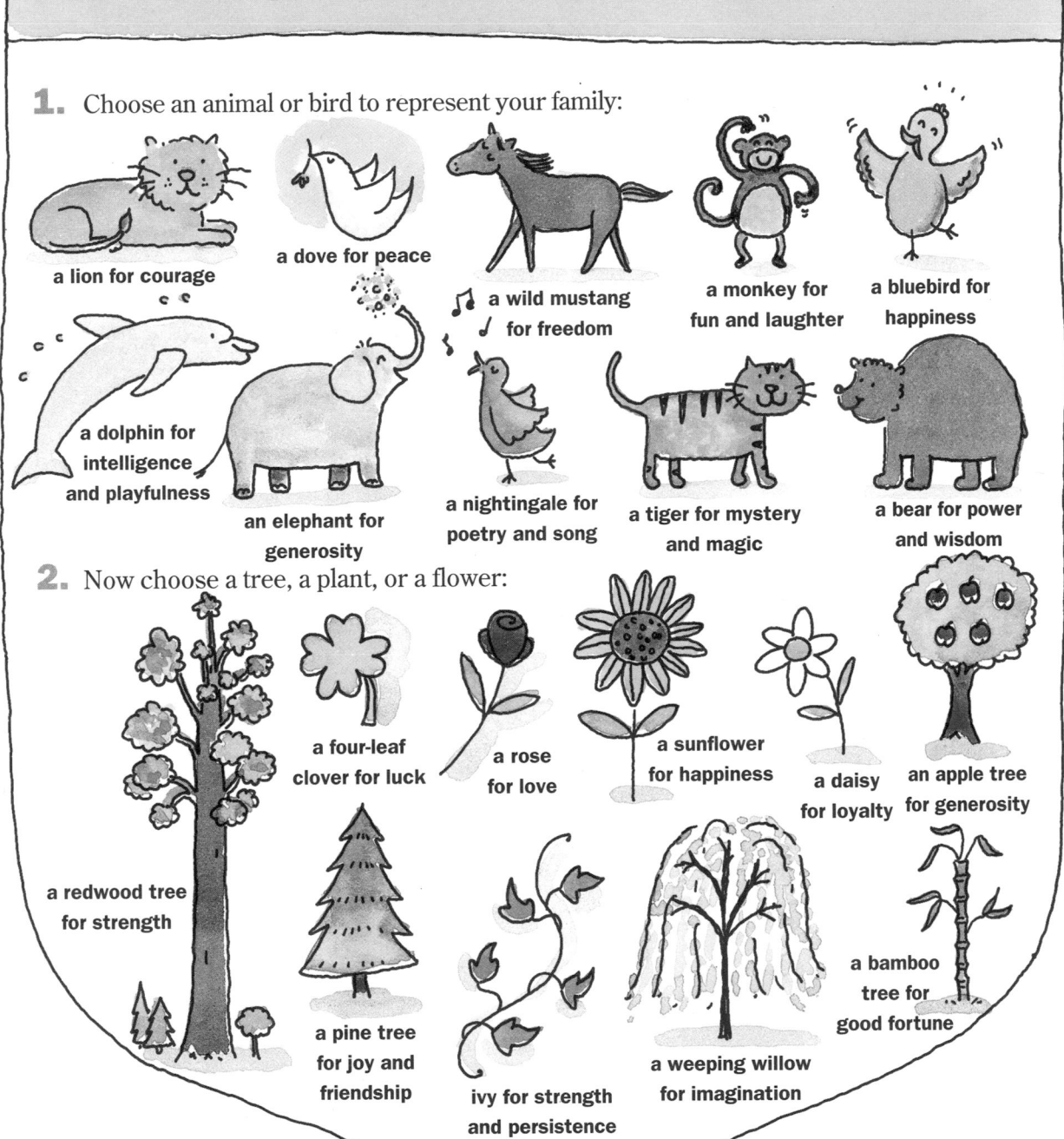

a lion for courage

a dove for peace

a wild mustang for freedom

a monkey for fun and laughter

a bluebird for happiness

a dolphin for intelligence and playfulness

an elephant for generosity

a nightingale for poetry and song

a tiger for mystery and magic

a bear for power and wisdom

2. Now choose a tree, a plant, or a flower:

a redwood tree for strength

a four-leaf clover for luck

a rose for love

a sunflower for happiness

a daisy for loyalty

an apple tree for generosity

a pine tree for joy and friendship

ivy for strength and persistence

a weeping willow for imagination

a bamboo tree for good fortune

3. Choose two background colors:

- ● red for excitement
- ● blue for creativity
- ● purple for following your dreams
- ● green for tackling challenges
- ○ yellow for happiness

- ○ white for honesty
- ● gray for intelligence
- ● orange for enthusiasm
- ● brown for dependability
- ● pink for caring for the feelings of others

4. Write your family motto:

Silly, Sillier, and Silliest   Peace + Love

Adventure, Excitement, and Courage

Pizza, Pizza, Pizza!

We Love Cookies!   Fun and Laughter

Truth, Honor, and Loyalty

friends and family forever

_____ family rules!

Draw your family's new coat of arms here!

Road Trip

It's time to hit the road for your family vacation! Find your family's **dream vacation** by picking the answers that fit your family best.

1. Mom and Dad announce a Family Fun Saturday! Your family . . .

   a. grabs your water bottles and heads to a nearby nature trail for a long hike.

   b. heads to the theater for a monster movie fest! Pass the popcorn, Dad.

   c. visits the local art museum, then goes out to dinner.

   d. splashes your way to the community pool for family swim time.

2. Ugh! Mom just let you know that this Saturday will be Family Clean-Up Day. Which of the following best describes your family?

   a. We draw straws for the best jobs in the backyard, while the losers get stuck with the indoor chores.

   b. It's a race! Whoever finishes their chores first gets to choose tonight's movie.

   c. We blast music or books on tape to make the chores go faster.

   d. We laze around for half the morning, then get to work. What's the big rush?

3. Your town's annual Fun Festival is this weekend. In between bites of funnel cake and cotton candy, your family . . .

a. zeros in on the petting zoo. Those baby animals are so cute!

b. heads straight for the rides, hoping they're bigger and scarier than last year's.

c. takes in the talent show. Maybe your neighbor will sing again this year.

d. sits back and people-watches while enjoying the sunshine.

4. Peek in your family's closets. Which of these types of shoes are you most likely to find?

a. hiking boots

b. sandals

c. comfy walking shoes

d. flip-flops

5. Your favorite item of clothing is . . .

a. a pair of cargo shorts with lots of pockets for my gear.

b. a logo T-shirt with a colorful picture of a place I've visited.

c. a pair of cool capri pants I can wear anywhere.

d. my sunglasses to keep the sun out of my eyes.

6. If your family could live anywhere, you'd choose . . .

    a. a tree house on a mountaintop.

    b. a castle in a magical kingdom.

    c. a penthouse apartment in a big city.

    d. a cottage on the beach.

7. It's the Family Olympics! Which of these sports will have your family going for the gold?

    a. Mountain climbing. The rougher the terrain, the better.

    b. Sidewinders, ollies, and kickflips. Extreme skateboarding!

    c. Hmmm. Is Monopoly a sport?

    d. Bring on the waves! We'd take the gold in boogie-boarding.

8. It's time for lunch and your stomach is rumbling! Choose one of these feasts for your family.

    a. Hot dogs roasted over a campfire, followed by s'mores for dessert. Yum!

    b. Something fast and on the run. Who wants to interrupt fun time for food?

    c. We love to try foods from different cultures, like Thai and Japanese, at cool new restaurants.

    d. If we weren't human, we'd be mermaids. We'll dine on the seafood feast!

Answers

Mostly b's
Thrills and Chills!
Roller coasters! Monster movie fests! Your family loves thrills and excitement and is happiest when you're on the run. A theme park is the perfect place for you to chill out this summer. Don't forget to give yourself some time to relax!

Mostly a's
Nature Lovers
Your family loves fresh air, physical challenges, and exploring the great outdoors. Grab your sleeping bags and your compass, and get ready to tell ghost tales around the campfire on your summer adventure!

Mostly c's
City Slickers
Your family enjoys art, music, and other cultural attractions—not to mention the hustle and bustle of a big city! Grab a guidebook and don't forget to wear your comfy walking shoes for your exotic big-city adventure.

Mostly d's
Beachcombers
Your family loves the feel of sand between your toes and the soothing sound of ocean waves hitting the shore. Don't forget to pack the sunscreen and the Frisbee when you head for your relaxing vacation at the beach!

Casting Call

TV producers are searching your town for the perfect family to star in a new **reality show.** Find out if your family's ready for prime time!

1. If your family won a dream vacation, which would you choose?

a. a deserted island. You'd test yourselves against the elements—and win!

b. herding cattle on a wild west dude ranch. So what if the odds are 500 cows to 4 humans?

c. a shopping spree at the world's biggest mall!

d. a fancy resort with spa treatments and lots of live entertainment

e. a trip to New York City and a chance to meet the rich and famous

2. Which one of these creative science projects would your family take on to earn a blue ribbon?

a. creating a challenging game for the judges to play, pitting one against the other

b. an experiment to determine if scorpions survive longer on a diet of spiders or a diet of insects

c. designing the house of the future—complete with robot maids, floating walls, and TVs that automatically tune in to your favorite programs

d. a song and dance number about all the cool things science does for us

e. a high-tech invention—like a music player so small, it'll fit inside your ear—that'll make us rich

3. If your family worked together, which of these jobs would you be best at?

   a. adventure travel guides, leading people through rushing rapids and tropical rain forests

   b. wildlife warriors, wrangling crocodiles and protecting wildlife

   c. interior decorators—give us a couple of days and we'll create a home paradise

   d. entertainers at a theme park. I'd be the princess. My brother could be the wolf.

   e. creating cool new products for a toy company

4. Which one of these pizza toppings is your family's pick?

   a. cheese. Plain pizza is supreme.

   b. mushrooms and sprouts. What? Fungi are yummy.

   c. color-coordinated red and green peppers

   d. sweet, exotic pineapple. I hear all the celebrities order their pizza that way.

   e. What's tonight's special? Pepperoni?

5. Your family's favorite method of transportation is . . .

   a. our own two feet—we're hikers.

   b. a helicopter.

   c. a car with a big trunk—to hold our shopping bags!

   d. a white stretch limo.

   e. a private jet.

6. It's Family Day at the State Fair! You . . .

a. enter the pole-climbing competition.

b. head straight for the haunted house exhibit.

c. enter the fashion design contest with your latest stylin' creation.

d. find the bandstand and check out the musical acts.

e. get a permit to set up a cream puff stand.

7. Your family's best quality is . . .

a. our strength and determination. When we start something, we finish it.

b. our bravery. We're always coming up with new, exciting adventures.

c. our creativity. We love to find and make beautiful things for our home and for friends and family.

d. our sense of humor. We love to entertain at parties and crack everyone up.

e. our competitive spirit. We're strong contenders, no matter what the challenge.

8. Before you head home, it's time for the rides. Which would you take on first?

a. a screaming-fast roller coaster. The first seat, of course.

b. the Tunnel of Fear—bring on the monsters!

c. the Ferris wheel, so we can view the entire layout from up high!

d. We'd skip the rides and head straight for the karaoke booth.

e. the carousel, where we can ride around in style.

Answers

Mostly a's
Island Castaways!
Bring on the desert island. You're great at roughing it in the wilderness, psyching out the competition, and winning rewards. You're ready to face the ultimate survival challenge on *Island Castaways*.

Mostly b's
Family Fear Fest
Whether you're jumping out of helicopters, wrangling crocodiles, or staring down hungry scorpions, your family is ready to face your fears and win on the next episode of *Family Fear Fest!* Just hope you don't have to eat any worms—yuck!

Mostly c's
Makeover Madness
You're creative and colorful. You know how to create homes that are beautiful and comfortable. As the stars of *Makeover Madness*, you'd make your own—and other people's—dreams come true.

Mostly d's
Family Pop Stars
You can sing. You can dance. You love to entertain. And you're ready to hear yourself on the radio! Don't forget to thank your fans when you win *Family Pop Stars* and your song is number one on the music charts!

Mostly e's
Family Business Tycoons
Ka-ching! Your family would love to zip around in your corporate jet and live the high life. You've got the drive and determination to make any business a success. You're the next billionaire winners of *Family Business Tycoons!*

Time Travel

Is your family better suited to **cross the prairie** in a covered wagon or **zip past the stars** in a spaceship? Step into the Family Time Machine to find out.

1. It's time for your annual trek to visit your cousins. You'd rather . . .

a. take a leisurely car trip, stopping at sights along the way.

b. hop on an airplane and get there fast.

2. When you can't see your friends and family in person, you'd rather stay in touch . . .

a. with cards and letters.

b. with e-mails and text messages.

3. On your family's summer vacation, you'd rather . . .

a. go camping in a national park, cooking over an open fire and sleeping under the stars.

b. go to space camp and learn how to be astronauts.

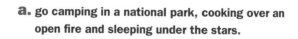

4. When it comes to food, your family would rather . . .

a. catch your own fish and grow your own vegetables.

b. buy frozen food that you can zap in the microwave.

5. When it comes to music, your family . . .

   a. likes live performances best—especially when you play your own instruments.

   b. bobs around to the beat of your personal portable music devices.

6. You'd rather live in . . .

   a. a log cabin out in the country.

   b. a luxury high-rise in the big city.

7. When it comes to arts and crafts, you . . .

   a. love to try things like candle-making and knitting.

   b. wonder why people make things when they're so easy to buy.

8. When it comes to the latest technology gizmo, you . . .

   a. wait and see how popular and useful it is before getting one of your own.

   b. run right out and buy one—the more blinking lights the better.

9. Your family likes to do your back-to-school shopping . . .

   a. in a big store with clothes, school supplies, and even lunch fixings all in one place.

   b. by clicking "send" and having it delivered straight to your door.

10. When it comes to chores, your family . . .

    a. rolls up your sleeves and gets to work.

    b. kicks up your heels and dreams of the days when robots will do all the dirty work.

11. When it comes to reading material, you prefer . . .

    a. stories based on history, like *Little House on the Prairie*.

    b. science fiction stories set in the future, like *A Wrinkle in Time*.

Answers

Mostly **a's**

Your family longs for a **simpler life.** You'd love to travel back in time to the days of the pioneers! You'd rather shop in a small general store, live off the land, and go to a one-room schoolhouse than rely on modern technology to fulfill your needs. Your pioneer spirit inspires you to roll up your sleeves and tackle challenges with a can-do attitude.

Mostly **b's**

Your family loves **modern conveniences** and being on the cutting edge of technology. You'd fit right in to the year 2115 or 2500! You don't see any reason to fend for yourselves if modern technology can make your lives easier. You love to try new things and dream about the future. Your adventurous spirit inspires you to leap into the future and new experiences with confidence.

Did you have a mix of a's and b's? Maybe today, with its mix of old and new, is exactly the right time for you.

What's in a Name?

Ask family members for their answers to the questions below to come up with new names for your "famous" gang!

Rodeo Rider

Are you a Wyoming Chaps, an Arizona Lasso, or a Dakota Saddle?

Your **favorite Western state**
+ your **favorite piece of cowboy gear**
(like saddle, spurs, boots, hat, lasso, chaps)
= your **rodeo name.**

List your family's rodeo names here:

....

....

Olympic Athlete

Michelle Panther? Lance Wildcat? Venus Warrior?

The first name of
your **favorite sports star**
+ your **favorite team**
= your **Olympic athlete name.**

List your family's Olympic athlete names. What sports would those gold-winners play?

....

....

Cartoon Character

Sneezy Indigo? Dopey Scarlet? Sleepy Asparagus?

Your favorite one of the seven dwarves
+ your favorite crayon color
= your cartoon character name.

List your family's cartoon names.

....

....

....

....

Movie Star Name

Are you a Frisky Maple, a Molly Cheesespring, or a Fluffy River?

Your first pet
+ the street you grew up on
= your movie star name!

List your family's movie star names below. What kinds of movies would they star in?

....

....

....

....

Animal Crackers

Poof! A fairy godmother just waved her **magic wand** and turned everyone in your family into a **different animal.** Would your sister be a sheep? Your father an owl? What animal would you be?

Canary: loves to sing and dance

Squirrel: "squirrels" things away—a collector

Penguin: creative and warmhearted

Lion: loud, with a big roar

Eagle: talented and confident

Sheep: puts the family's needs first

Rabbit: quiet and shy

Cat: independent and mysterious

Raccoon: eats everything in sight

Hamster: busy, busy, busy —all the time

Owl: wise, and likes to stay up late

Dog: cheerful and easygoing

Deer: loves to run and jump

Create your animal family here:

....
(Family Member)   (Animal)

....
(Family Member)   (Animal)

....
(Family Member)   (Animal)

....
(Family Member)   (Animal)

....
(Family Member)   (Animal)

....
(Family Member)   (Animal)

Draw your new animal family portrait!

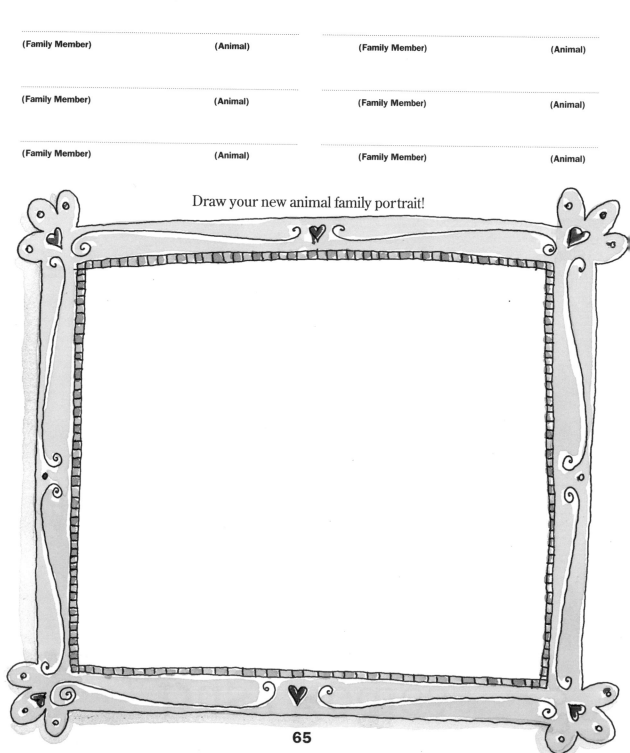

Busy Bodies

Your town is having its annual Founders' Day Picnic in the park. After a day filled with food, fun, and games, will your family go home feeling **healthy and fit** or **stuffed and tired?**

1. Your family is supposed to arrive early to set up booths and picnic tables. You oversleep, so for breakfast you . . .

  a. grab a doughnut and run. We don't have time to eat.

  b. eat a banana. We'll make up for it with a healthy breakfast tomorrow.

  c. stop and eat a healthy breakfast. Food is fuel. We can't work without it.

2. The park is half a mile away. How does your family get there?

  a. It's half a mile! Dad drives. Who wants to be tuckered out before the fun starts?

  b. The sun is shining and all the streets have sidewalks— we enjoy the walk!

  c. It's a beautiful day! We in-line skate or ride our bikes.

3. Your family's contribution to the eats is . . .

    a. a gooey, nutty batch of chocolate brownies.

    b. hamburgers and hot dogs for the grill.

    c. corn on the cob and a green salad.

4. When it's time to eat, you fill your plates with . . .

    a. everything in sight! Well, except for that salad. We have to save room to sample all the desserts.

    b. our favorite foods, followed by one or two of those gooey, nutty brownies.

    c. food? We were having so much fun, we forgot to eat until we were absolutely starving.

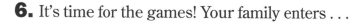

5. Food fights! Which one of these contests would your family win?

    a. the pie-eating contest. We're the hands-down winners. Gulp.

    b. Move over, everyone, the hot-dog-eating champs are here. Burp.

    c. the watermelon-seed-spitting contest

6. It's time for the games! Your family enters . . .

    a. Enter? Isn't it naptime? We're too full to run around.

    b. the three-legged race. Hey, Dad, we're supposed to go forward, not backward.

    c. the family triathlon—swimming and biking, followed by a relay race. Whew!

7. Which one of these booths would your family manage?

    a. the bake sale. We might as well work where we spend the most money.

    b. the dunking booth. Hit the bull's-eye and underwater we go!

    c. the climbing demonstration on the rock formation

8. At the charity raffle, your family hopes to win . . .

    a. the big-screen TV and DVD player.

    b. a pool table for the basement.

    c. a set of mountain bikes for the whole family.

9. An old-fashioned square dance ends the festivities. Your family . . .

    a. calls the moves from the stage. Swing your partner and do-si-do!

    b. hits the floor for a few dances before heading home.

    c. leads every dance. Who else has the energy to demonstrate all those fancy steps?

Answers

Mostly a's

Couch Potatoes

You do have the best brownie recipe in town, but when you fill your bodies with empty calories, you end up watching the fun from the sidelines. Take a walk after dinner, ease up on the desserts, and add a little green stuff—like salad—to your diet. Not only will you feel healthier and have more energy, but your brains will work better, too. The next time somebody says "swing your partner," you'll be ready to do-si-do.

Mostly b's

Armchair Broccoli

You eat healthy foods sometimes and usually get some physical exercise, but you're just as likely to veg on the couch as you are to take the dog for a walk after school. Try new things like yoga or ice-skating until you find a fitness routine that works for you. And, as long as it's an extra-special treat, that second brownie isn't a problem—occasionally. Remember to eat foods that give you the vitamins and minerals that your bodies really need, and you'll all have the energy to finish that race.

Mostly c's

Mighty Spinach

Wow! Your family is strong and healthy. You never ride when you can walk, and you dance right past those pies searching for the healthy watermelon. But sometimes you get so caught up in sports and games that you forget to eat, which can lead to giant energy slumps. Stop and refuel every now and then, and remember that it's O.K. to enjoy a gooey chocolate brownie after a fun-filled, active day.

Fact or Fiction?

Write your initials in a box after each statement that is **true** about you.
Make sure everyone in your family fills it out!

I'm afraid of clowns.

Cats make me sneeze.

I can tap-dance.

I've stuffed a turkey.

I've reeled in a fish.

I've screamed on a roller coaster.

I've been on TV.

I've won a race.

I've seen a whale.

I've painted somebody else's toenails.

I've won a spelling bee.

I've pretended my hairbrush was a microphone.

I've acted in a play.

I've had my picture in the newspaper.

I've stepped in dog poop.

I've spent the night under the stars.

I've climbed a tree.

I've seen a Great Lake.

I've ridden a horse.

I've read a book in one day.

Family Awards
& World Records

Who can eat the **most pieces of pizza** in one sitting? Who's the **best barbecue chef?** Who's the **biggest computer hog?** Fill out the award certificates below, and make up some new categories of your own!

The
....
(last name)

Family World Record

for

Most Cookies
Eaten in One Sitting

is hereby awarded to

....
(name)

on

....
(date)

by

....
(signature)

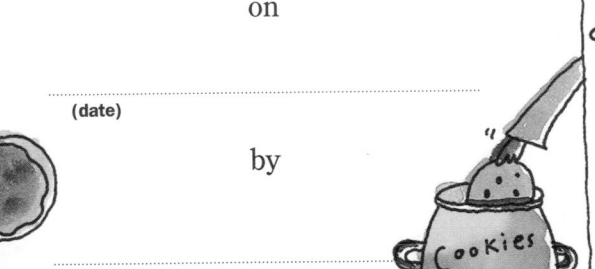

The
....
(last name)

Family Award

for

Best Barbecue
Chef in Town

is hereby awarded to

....
(name)

on

....
(date)

by

....
(signature)

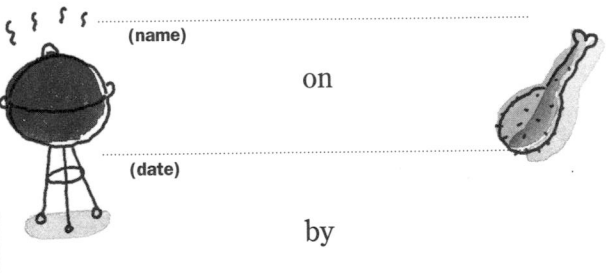

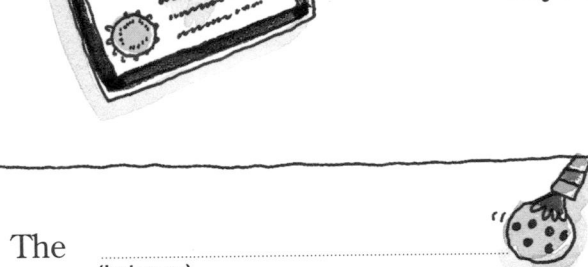

The
(last name)

Family Award

for

Biggest Computer Hog

is hereby awarded to

(name)

on

(date)

by

(signature)

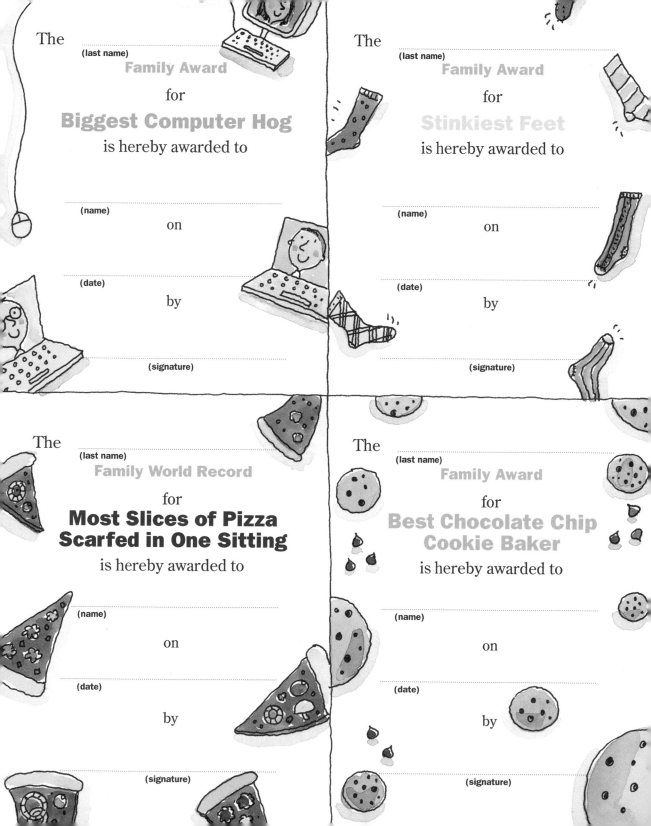

The
(last name)

Family Award

for

Stinkiest Feet

is hereby awarded to

(name)

on

(date)

by

(signature)

The
(last name)

Family World Record

for

**Most Slices of Pizza
Scarfed in One Sitting**

is hereby awarded to

(name)

on

(date)

by

(signature)

The
(last name)

Family Award

for

**Best Chocolate Chip
Cookie Baker**

is hereby awarded to

(name)

on

(date)

by

(signature)

The `....(last name)....` Family Award

for

Funniest Joke Teller

is hereby awarded to

`....(name)....`

on

`....(date)....`

by

`....(signature)....`

The `....(last name)....` Family Award

for

Messiest Bedroom

is hereby awarded to

`....(name)....`

on

`....(date)....`

by

`....(signature)....`

The `....(last name)....` Family Award

for

Most Competitive Board Game Player

is hereby awarded to

`....(name)....`

on

`....(date)....`

by

`....(signature)....`

The `....(last name)....` Family Award

for

Most Creative Sandwich Maker

is hereby awarded to

`....(name)....`

on

`....(date)....`

by

`....(signature)....`

The _(last name)_

Family Award

for _____

is hereby awarded to

(name)

on

(date)

by

(signature)

The _(last name)_

Family Award

for _____

is hereby awarded to

(name)

on

(date)

by

(signature)

The _(last name)_

Family World Record

for _____

is hereby awarded to

(name)

on

(date)

by

(signature)

The _(last name)_

Family World Record

for _____

is hereby awarded to

(name)

on

(date)

by

(signature)

Personal Poem

Write your family's name in cool, colorful letters, and then turn it into a Personal Poem! Check out our sample for ideas.

F is for **Friendship.** We're more than family—we're friends, too.

A is for **Always.** We'll always be a loving family.

M is for **Miles**—for the family members who live far away but are in our hearts.

I is for **Inspiration.** We inspire each other to be the best we can be.

L is for **Love and Laughter.** We have both!

Y is for **Yay!** I'm so happy to be a member of this family!

Family Matters

Isn't it cool that there are so many different kinds of families? Circle the things that you think are important to make a happy family.

Talented

Fun

Kind

Understanding

Loving

Smart

Interesting

Courageous

Loyal

Tell us what your family
liked best about
The Family Quiz Book.

a. Quizzes

b. Family Fill-ins

c. Activities
(Family Crest,
Family Tree,
Personal Poem)

d. Family Awards

e. All of it

Write to :

Family Quiz Editor

American Girl

8400 Fairway Place

Middleton, WI 53562

Here are some other American Girl books you might like:

 **Tear Up This Book!** The sticker, stencil, stationery, games, crafts, doodle, and journal book for girls! By Keri Smith

❏ I read it.

 **What a Girl Loves** Puzzle Book

❏ I read it.

 **Puzzle Crazy**

❏ I read it.

 **The Quiz Book** Clues to You & Your Friends, Too!

❏ I read it.

 **The Quiz Book 2** More Secrets Revealed!

❏ I read it.

 **The Quiz Book 3** Three Times the Fun!

❏ I read it.

 **The POP Quiz Book** Tons of Trivia!

❏ I read it.